# Keto Diet Des

*Ketogenic Diet Desserts That You MUST Prepare Before Any Other!*

# Introduction

If you've recently started following the Ketogenic diet, it is easy to think you cannot have sweet and savory treats to take care of your sweet tooth. Think about it; with the Ketogenic diet, carbs are greatly limited. And one of the ingredients that's specifically not allowed is wheat and all its products.

How are you supposed to have treats and which ones are you supposed to take considering that many of the desserts you are used to have wheat and other ingredients that are clearly off limits when following the keto diet?

Well, I know you've tried to search for keto desserts online but you can agree with me that the sheer number of dessert options can be overwhelming. This book seeks to solve the problem of overwhelm by giving you 50+ dessert options that you MUST start with before anything else.

**More precisely, this book covers the following:**

- Ice creams and yogurt recipes

- **Chocolate and candy recipes**

- Cake recipes

- **Bread and pie recipes**

- Brownie and cookie recipes

- **Custard and pudding recipes**

- And much, much more!

*Keto Diet Desserts*

The book takes a no BS approach to keto desserts. I know you are looking to prepare desserts immediately and I will give you just that! You can prepare a new recipe every week for a year with the recipes in this book! Let it save you the trouble of having to figure out which recipe to prepare from the hundreds or perhaps 1000s of recipes you may find online.

## Your Free Gifts

As a way of thanking you for the purchase, I'd like to offer you 2 complimentary gifts:

- **How To Get Through Any Weight Loss Plateau While On The Ketogenic Diet:** The title is self-explanatory; if you are struggling with getting off a weight loss plateau while on the Keto diet, you will find this free gift very eye opening on what has been ailing you. Grab your copy now by clicking/tapping here or simply enter http://bit.ly/2fantonpubketo into your browser.

- **5 Pillar Life Transformation Checklist:** This short book is about life transformation, presented in bit size pieces for easy implementation. I believe that without such a checklist, you are likely to have a hard time implementing anything in this book and any other thing you set out to do religiously and sticking to it for the long haul. It doesn't matter whether your goals relate to weight loss, relationships, personal finance, investing, personal development, improving communication in your family, your overall health, finances, improving your sex life, resolving issues in your relationship, fighting PMS successfully, investing, running a successful business, traveling etc. With a checklist like this one, you can bet that anything you do will seem a lot easier to implement until the end. Therefore, even if you don't continue reading this book, at least read the one thing that will help you in every other aspect of your life. Grab your copy now by clicking/tapping here or simply enter http://bit.ly/2fantonfreebie into your browser. Your life will never be the same again (if you implement what's in this book), I promise.

**PS:** I'd like your feedback. If you are happy with this book, please leave a review on Amazon.

# Table of Contents

**Introduction** ---------------------------------------------- 2

**Your Free Gifts** ---------------------------------------- 4

**Ice Creams & Yoghurts** ---------------------------- 13

*Green Tea Ice Cream* ------------------------------ 13

*Chocolate Ice Cream* ------------------------------ 15

*Avocado Sorbet* ----------------------------------- 16

*Keto Fat Bomb Ice Cream* ----------------------- 18

*Low Carb Ice Cream Bars* ---------------------- 20

*Swirl Frozen Yogurt* ------------------------------- 23

*Peach Cream Dessert* ----------------------------- 25

*Dairy Free Coffee Ice Cream* --------------------- 27

*Keto Ice Cream* ----------------------------------- 29

*Keto Vanilla Ice Cream* --------------------------- 31

**Chocolate and Candy** ------------------------- 33

*Chocolate Almond Fat Bomb* --------------------- 33

*Chocolate Slushies* -------------------------------- 34

*Keto Ferrero Rocher* ------------------------------ 36

*Keto Chocolate Fondue* --------------------------- 38

*Healthy Dark Chocolate* -------------------------- 40

*Berries with Chocolate Ganache* ---------------- 42

*White Chocolate Fat Bomb* --------------------- 43

Keto Macaroon Fat Bombs ---------------------- 44
Keto Chocolate Pots de Crème ------------------ 46
Keto Chocolate Soufflé --------------------------- 48

## Cakes -------------------------------------------------- 50
Low Carb Slow Cooker Cheesecake -------------- 50
Crust-less Keto Cheesecake ---------------------- 52
Keto Dark Chocolate Cake ----------------------- 54
Keto Chocolate Molten Lava Cake --------------- 56
Blueberry Lemon Custard Cake ------------------ 58
Almond Sponge Cake with Lemon Curd --------- 60
Almond flour Mocha Fudge Cake ---------------- 63
Instant Pot Brownie Cake ------------------------ 65
Crock Pot Fudge ----------------------------------- 67
Almond and Coconut Muffin --------------------- 69

## Bread and Pies ---------------------------------------- 71
Almond Flour Goji Buns -------------------------- 71
Sugar-free Mud Pie ------------------------------- 73
Blackberry Clafouti ------------------------------- 76
Strawberry Cream Pie ---------------------------- 78
Pecan Pie ------------------------------------------- 80
Keto Pistachio Pudding Pie ---------------------- 83
Easy & Delicious Keto Pie ------------------------ 85
Dream Pie ------------------------------------------ 87

Keto Cream Pie ---------------------------------- 89

## Brownies and Cookies ------------------------- 92

Nut Free Keto Brownie-------------------------- 92

Keto Avocado Brownies ------------------------ 94

Keto Peanut Butter Cookies -------------------- 96

Keto Fudgy Brownie Cookies-------------------- 98

Almond Butter Brownie Cookies--------------- 100

No Bake Brownie Cookies ---------------------- 102

Skillet Brownies---------------------------------- 104

Collagen Protein Brownies --------------------- 106

Chocolate Keto Brownies ---------------------- 108

Flourless Keto Brownies -------------------------110

## Custards and Puddings----------------------- 112

Keto Chocolate Mousse -------------------------112

Almond Chia Seed Pudding ---------------------114

Keto Vanilla Custard ----------------------------116

Keto Baked Custard ----------------------------- 117

Low Carb Custard Lemon ----------------------119

Keto Custard ------------------------------------121

Keto Custard - Vanilla Flavor------------------ 123

Low Carb Vanilla Pudding -------------------- 125

## Conclusion-------------------------------------128

## Do You Like My Book & Approach To Publishing? --------------------------------------- **129**

*1: First, I'd Love It If You Leave a Review of This Book on Amazon.* ---------------------------------*129*

*2: Check Out My Other Keto Diet Books* --------*129*

*3: Let's Get In Touch* ------------------------------ *131*

*4: Grab Some Freebies On Your Way Out; Giving Is Receiving, Right?* ------------------------------ *131*

*5: Suggest Topics That You'd Love Me To Cover To Increase Your Knowledge Bank.* -------------*132*

## PSS: Let Me Also Help You Save Some Money! ------------------------------------------ **133**

**Copyright 2019 by Fantonpublishers.com - All rights reserved.**

**PS:**

I have special interest in the Ketogenic diet. My wife has been following the Ketogenic diet and I can honestly say that the journey has been amazing. The diet works. And this is why I have committed to writing and publishing as many of the Ketogenic diet books as possible to give readers different options as far as the Ketogenic diet is concerned.

For instance, I have Ketogenic diet books exclusively dedicated for:

- Breakfast
- Main Meals
- Snacks
- Desserts
- Appetizers
- Soups
- Vegetarians
- Crockpot/slow cooker users
- Instant pot users
- Air fryer users
- People who are on the Paleo diet
- People who are following intermittent fasting

- People who are following carb cycling

And much more.

You can check out my [Ketogenic Diet Books fan page shop](#) for more of the books, as I continue publishing more and more. If you want me to add your category of the Ketogenic diet books that I have published so far, make sure to send me a message. I will do the heavy lifting for you and get back to you with a book that you will love.

You could also subscribe to my newsletter to receive updates whenever I have something new: [http://bit.ly/2Cketodietfanton](http://bit.ly/2Cketodietfanton).

# Ice Creams & Yoghurts

## Green Tea Ice Cream

*Prep Time 10 minutes*

*Cook Time 30 minutes*

*Total Time 40 minutes*

*Servings 5*

*Ingredients*

1 1/2 cups heavy cream

1/2 cup almond milk, unsweetened

1/2 cup Swerve

4 green tea bags

1/3 cup boiling water

*Directions*

1. Begin by putting the tea bags in the boiling water in a cup.

2. Allow to steep as required, for about 5 minutes or so.

3. Once done, simply squeeze the tea from individual teabags and then discard them.

4. Add in a sweetener of choice such as swerve to the hot tea. Set it aside until it is cool enough to handle.

5. Once cooled, stir in the unsweetened almond milk along with the heavy cream.

6. Pour the mixture into the canister of an ice cream maker and make the ice cream according to manufacturer's instructions.

7. Serve the ice cream instantly for best flavor and store any remainder in the freezer. To serve the frozen ice cream you should thaw it for a few minutes before serving.

8. If you don't have a churning machine, you can alternatively whip the mixture using an electric beater until it has thickened and then store in the freezer.

9. Keep stirring the mixture at intervals of about 20 minutes up until you have the consistency of ice cream.

*Calories 249, Carbs 2.1g, Protein 1.5g, Fat 25.6g*

## Chocolate Ice Cream

*Prep Time: 20 minutes*

*Cook Time: 0 minutes*

*Total Time: 20 minutes*

*Serves: 2*

*Ingredients*

1 teaspoon organic vanilla extract

1/4 cup dark cocoa powder

1/3 cup Confectioner's Style Swerve

2 organic free-range eggs

1 cup heavy cream

Pinch of unrefined sea salt

*Directions*

1. Put each of these ingredients in a deep narrow bowl.

2. Stir using a spoon and then mix with your electric mixer until well blended.

3. Pour the cream in the ice cream machine and churn according to the manufacturer's directions.

*Calories 532, Carbs 5g, Protein 13g, Fat 51g*

## Avocado Sorbet

*Prep time: 5 minutes*

*Cook time: 15 minutes*

*Total time: 20 minutes*

*Serves: 5*

*Ingredients*

½ teaspoon Celtic sea salt

1 teaspoon mango extract or other extract

2 tablespoons lime juice

¾ cup Swerve or other sweetener

2 ripe avocados

2 cups almond milk, unsweetened

*Directions*

1. Put all the ingredients in a food processor and process until smooth.

2. Move the mixture to the chilled container of an ice cream maker and churn as required.

3. Transfer the ice cream to a chilled container and store in a freezer.

4. In case the sorbet is not as sweet as desired, adjust the amount of the natural sweetener and then refreeze it.

*Keto Diet Desserts*

*Calories 146, Carbs 8.2g, Protein 2g, Fat 13.2g*

## Keto Fat Bomb Ice Cream

*Prep time: 10 minutes*

*Cook time: 60 minutes*

*Total time: 1 hour 10 minutes*

*Serves: 5*

*Ingredients*

8-10 ice cubes

2 teaspoons vanilla bean powder

¼ cup MCT oil

1/3 cup xylitol or 15-20 drops of alcohol-free stevia

1/3 cup melted coconut oil

1/3 cup melted cacao butter

4 yolks from pastured eggs

4 whole pastured eggs

*Directions*

1. Add all of the ingredients into the jug of a Vitamix or any other high-powered blender apart from the ice cubes.

2. Process on high speed until creamy, or for about 2 minutes or so.

3. Remove the top portion of the lid with the blender still running and add in all the ice cubes one at a time.

4. Let the blender run for about 10 seconds between each of the ice cube. If your blender has no hole on the lid, turn it off with each addition of the ice cube one piece at a time.

5. As soon as you have added all ice cubes, pour the mixture into the ice cream machine and churn on high speed for around 20 to 30 minutes.

6. Alternatively, transfer the mixture into a 9 by 5 loaf pan and keep in the freezer for approximately 30 minutes. Stir and repeat for another 2 to 3 hours until you get your preferred consistency.

7. Serve it soft or instead scoop into a 9 by 5 inch pan and keep frozen for another 45 minutes. Store any leftovers covered in the freezer for less than 7 days.

*Calories 497, Carbs 4.6g, Protein 9.3g, Fat 48.8g*

## Low Carb Ice Cream Bars

*Prep Time: 15 minutes*

*Cook Time: 15 minutes*

*Cool Time: 4 hours*

*Total Time: 4 hours 30 minutes*

*Serves 8-12*

*Ingredients*

2 ounces sugar-free chocolate

1/2 teaspoon vanilla extract

3 egg yolks

1 teaspoon instant espresso powder

1/2 cup Swerve Sweetener

2 teaspoons grass-fed gelatin

3 cups full fat coconut milk, divided

*Directions*

1. Add half a cup of coconut milk along with some gelatin in a medium saucepan. Allow to stand for a few minutes then set the heat to medium. Whisk the mixture until gelatin has dissolved.

2. Add in the rest of the coconut milk, instant coffee and the sweetener and stir the mixture until the coffee and the

sweetener dissolve. The temperature on the instant read thermometer should be at approximately 175 degree F.

3. Now in a medium sized bowl, whisk the 3 egg yolks for a few seconds. Add in a cup of the hot coffee and coconut milk mixture and continue to whisk to temper the yolks.

4. Whisk this egg yolk mixture back into cream as you continue to whisk constantly.

5. Cook the mixture until it reaches 180 degrees F on the instant read thermometer.

6. Remove the mixture from heat and put it over an ice bath, let it cool until no longer hot to touch, or for up to 15 minutes.

7. Stir in the vanilla extract and distribute the mixture among 12 small Popsicle molds. Freeze for around 40 minutes, and then insert a wooden stick around 2/3 into each of them.

8. Freeze for 3 hours or so. Meanwhile melt the chocolate in a bowl placed over simmering water.

9. Once done, unmold the popsicles from the molds by running hot water over them for 20 to 30 seconds.

10. Set them on a waxed paper-lined baking sheet, and then return them into the freezer.

11. Hold each of the Popsicle over the bowl one at a time and drizzle with the chocolate, and turn to get all sides. Keep it the freezer and repeat the process with the rest of the popsicles.

*Keto Diet Desserts*

*Calories 235, Carbs 6g, Protein 3.8g, Fat 21.65g*

## Swirl Frozen Yogurt

*Prep Time: 15 minutes*

*Cook Time: 0 minutes*

*Total Time: 15 minutes*

*Servings: 6*

*Ingredients*

2 tablespoons powdered stevia

1 teaspoon vanilla liquid stevia

1 teaspoon vanilla extract

1 banana mashed

1/4 teaspoon salt

1/2 cup milk

2 cups plain Greek yogurt 2%

1/2 cup peanut butter no sugar added, if using

*Optional:*

2 tablespoons peanut butter

*Directions*

1. In a blender or mixer, blend all of the ingredients apart from the butter.

2. Pour the mixture into an ice cream maker and churn based on the manufacturer's instructions.

3. Stir and add in some peanut butter if using or instead top it onto each of the serving.

4. Serve or instead move to a shallow airtight container and keep it frozen for about 2 to 3 hours to harden.

5. Let it defrost for about 5 to 10 minutes before serving. In case you freeze it overnight, let it thaw for 30 minutes for easier scoping.

*Calories 201, Carbs 12g, Protein 13g, Fat 11g*

# Peach Cream Dessert

*Prep Time: 10 minutes*

*Cook Time: 10 minutes*

*Total Time: 20 minutes*

*Serves 8*

*Ingredients*

1 tablespoon of raspberry syrup, sugar free

1 package peach Jell-O, sugar free

2 cups heavy whipping cream

*Directions*

1. In a glass cereal bowl, heat a cup of cream in your microwave, until it's extremely hot. This should take about for 2 minutes

2. Then in the hot cream, add in raspberry syrup and peach Jell-O and stir to mix until you dissolve the Jell-O fully. Allow it to cool to around 24 degrees Celsius(room temperature).

3. Now place the chilled cream in a well cooled metal bowl and then beat on low speed to gradually mix in the peach cream.

4. Beat on high speed to achieve a thick texture, and then put in the fridge to set.

*Keto Diet Desserts*

*Calories: 209.4, Carbs 1.7g, Protein 1.9g, Fat 22.0g*

# Dairy Free Coffee Ice Cream

*Prep Time: 30 minutes*

*Cook Time: 8 hour*

*Total Time: 8 hours 30 minutes*

*Serves: 8*

*Ingredients*

¼ teaspoon stevia extract

1 teaspoons organic vanilla extract

2 tablespoons raw coconut nectar

1 cup organic coffee, double strength

1/4 teaspoon sea salt

2 teaspoons gelatin, unflavored

48 tablespoons organic coconut milk

*Directions*

1. Into a medium saucepan, add the organic coffee and then simmer to reduce the amount to ½ cup.

2. Sprinkle the gelatin into the coffee and then warm it over low heat, until the gelatin fully dissolves. You don't need to stir.

3. Now in a blender, spoon all of your coffee mixture and then blend until it's smooth. Add the coconut nectar, stevia and sea salt and continue to blend.

4. Then add in vanilla, milk and continue to blend. Once done, pour into a bowl and cool for 6 hours while covered to get a custard-like substance.

5. Transfer into the freezer bowl of your ice cream maker and continue to make the ice cream based on the directions of the manufacturer. Freeze for about 2 hours until firm.

*Calories 178g, Carbs 10.9g, Protein 3.7g, Fat 15g*

# Keto Ice Cream

*Prep Time: 10 minutes*

*Cook Time: 0 minutes*

*Total Time: 10 minutes*

*Serves 4-5*

*Ingredients*

1 1/2 teaspoon vanilla bean paste or pure vanilla extract

1/8 teaspoon salt

1/3 cup erythritol, xylitol, or other natural sweetener

2 cups canned coconut milk, full fat

*Directions*

1. Stir the full-fat canned coconut milk with vanilla extract and salt.

2. In case you have an ice cream machine, churn the mixture based on the manufacturer's instructions.

3. If you do not have an ice cream machine, simply freeze the coconut milk and vanilla extract mixture in ice tube trays.

4. In a Vitamix or any other high-speed blender, blend the frozen cubes for a few seconds or instead thaw them for some time before processing in a regular food processor.

4. Serve or alternatively chill for an hour or so to get a firmer texture.

*Calories 184, Carbs 4.4g, Protein 1.8g, Fat 19.1g*

# Keto Vanilla Ice Cream

*Prep Time: 15 minutes*

*Cook Time: 15 minutes*

*Chilling Time: 5 hours*

*Total Time: 20 minutes*

*Serves 10*

*Ingredients*

2 teaspoons vanilla extract

480g heavy whipping cream

1/4 teaspoon xanthan gum

1/4 teaspoon kosher salt

135-150 g xylitol erythritol, to taste*

1 13.5-ounce can full fat coconut milk

1 vanilla bean (i.e. pod) or more vanilla extract

*Directions*

1. Begin by slicing up the vanilla bean and then using a knife scrape off the seeds from the bean.

2. Over medium heat, add in the vanilla bean with scraped seeds, sweetener, coconut milk and some salt to a saucepan.

3. Whisk the mixture until all the lumps from coconut milk have disappeared and you have a smooth mixture. Simmer the smooth mixture to help infuse the milk.

4. Once done, discard the vanilla bean and then sprinkle with xanthan gum gradually until well blended.

5. At this point, sieve the mixture to a bowl. Then using a layer of cling film (the saran wrap), cover the vanilla mixture.

6. Let the vanilla mixture cool fully until you have a thick and jelly-like consistency.

7. To a large chilled bowl, add in coconut cream or whipping cream and whip until you obtain soft peaks, and then add in vanilla extract to the vanilla bean mixture.

8. In case your mixture is too thick, add in additional coconut milk to thin it to your liking.

9. Move the ice cream to a container and seal it tight. Put the container in the freezer for about 4 to 6 hours or preferably overnight until frozen. Alternatively, churn it in an ice cream machine for just around 15 minutes!

10. The following day, remove the ice cream from the freezer about 10 to 20 minutes before serving. Scoop and enjoy!

*Calories 235, Carbs 2g, Protein 1g, Fat 25g*

# Chocolate and Candy

## Chocolate Almond Fat Bomb

*Prep Time: 5 minutes*

*Cook Time: 5 minutes*

*Total Time: 10 minutes*

*Serves: 15*

*Ingredients*

10-15 whole almonds

½ cup cacao powder

1 cup coconut oil

1/4 cup coconut flour

1 cup almond butter

*Directions*

1. In a saucepan, melt coconut oil and butter. Add in stevia, coconut flour and cacao powder and mix well.

2. Allow the mixture to cool down and then make 10 to 15 Ping-Pong sized balls from the batter.

3. Now stick an almond into each bomb and keep it refrigerated until ready to serve.

*Calories: 260, Carbs: 6g Protein: 4g, Fat: 26g*

## Chocolate Slushies

*Prep Time: 5 Minutes*

*Cook Time: 10 Minutes*

*Total Time: 15 minutes*

*Serves 4*

*Ingredients*

1 teaspoon vanilla extract

½ cup chocolate syrup, sugar free

2 tablespoons cocoa powder, unsweetened

1/2 cup tap water

1 cup heavy cream

*Directions*

1. Mix together chocolate syrup, cocoa powder, water and cream in a medium saucepan

2. Bring the mixture to a boil over medium heat and then lower the heat to low. Cook for about 5 minutes, while stirring occasionally.

3. After the five minutes, remove the mixture from heat and stir in vanilla. Now pour the mixture into ice cube trays and keep frozen for around 2 hours.

4. Move the cubes to a food processor and pulse until slushy and well chopped

*Calories 230, Carbs 8.3g, Protein 2.8g, Fat 22.4g*

# Keto Ferrero Rocher

*Prep Time: 10 minutes*

*Cook Time: 10 minutes*

*Total Time: 20 minutes*

*Serves: 12*

*Ingredients*

1/4 cup chopped hazelnuts

2 ounces chocolate bar, sugar free

12 hazelnuts

1/2 cup homemade nutella

*Directions*

1. First toast the hazelnuts in a skillet for a few minutes, or until fragrant.

2. Remove as much skin as you can remove then allow to cool. Keep the nutella in the fridge then scoop a teaspoon. Flatten it like a mini pancake.

3. Put the flattened nutella on a baking sheet that is coated with parchment paper.

4. Top with one of the toasted hazelnut, and then add a teaspoon of nutella. Now mold into a ball shape.

5. Prepare about 12 balls and keep them frozen. Meanwhile, melt the chocolate bar then stir in chopped hazelnuts. Mix well.

6. Pick one nutella ball and dip in the chocolate coating. Repeat for other balls.

7. Remove the balls using a fork then set on a baking sheet lined with parchment paper.

8. Do the same with the rest and refrigerate.

9. Wrap each of the balls in foil and keep in an airtight container. Keep in the fridge until ready to serve.

*Calories: 202, Carbs: 7.3g, Protein: 3.8g, Fat: 20.1g*

## Keto Chocolate Fondue

*Prep Time: 2 minutes*

*Cook Time: 10 minutes*

*Total Time: 12 minutes*

*Serves 2-4*

*Ingredients*

1 teaspoon Amaretto liquor

1 teaspoon coconut sugar

3.5 oz. fresh cream

3.5 oz. Swiss dark bittersweet chocolate 85%

*Directions*

1. Add 2 cups of water and a trivet or rack to a pressure cooker pot. Set aside.

2. Add the chocolate in large chunks in a heatproof container and obtain their weight.

3. Add same amount of sugar, fresh cream, liquor and spices if desired.

4. Lower the container into Instant Pot and lock the lid. Cook for 2 minutes on high pressure then quick release pressure.

5. Pull out the container using tongs and then stir the contents for a minute using a fork. Do this to create a thick dark-brown mixture.

6. Serve with strawberries sliced into bite-sizes.

*Calories 216, Carbs 6.5g, Protein 1.8g, Fat 20.3g*

## Healthy Dark Chocolate

*Prep Time: 15 minutes*

*Cook Time: 15 minutes*

*Total Time: 30 minutes*

*Makes 100 grams*

*Ingredients*

Seeds of 1 vanilla bean

2½ tablespoons cocoa powder

1½ tablespoons maple syrup

3½ tablespoons cocoa butter

*Directions*

1. Over low heat, melt cocoa butter in a small saucepan and then stir in vanilla bean seeds, cocoa powder and sugar-free maple syrup. Whisk the mixture until smooth.

2. Temper the chocolate using a candy thermometer. Heat to 120 degrees F and then cool in the fridge at 79 degrees F for 10-15 minutes. Ensure that you stir the contents every 5 minutes.

3. Once the time elapses, remove from the fridge and heat at a constant temperature of 87 degrees F.

4. Pour into the mold, cool and then store the chocolate in the fridge until ready to serve.

*Keto Diet Desserts*

*Calories 466, Carbs 11g, Protein 3.4g, Fat 50g*

## Berries with Chocolate Ganache

*Prep Time: 10 Minutes*

*Cook Time: 5 Minutes*

*Total Time: 15 Minutes*

*Serves 6*

*Ingredients*

2 cups fresh blueberries

1/3 cup heavy cream

2 cups red raspberries

1/2 teaspoons vanilla extract

8 oz. strawberries

8 ounce chocolate chips, sugar free

*Directions*

1. Mix the fruits and put the mixture into dessert bowls.

2. Heat the cream and chocolate over low heat until melted, or alternatively microwave for around 30 seconds.

3. Add the vanilla and stir to get a smooth consistency.

4. Cool slightly and serve.

*Calories 285.3, Carbs 17.6g, Protein 4g, Fat 17.6g*

# White Chocolate Fat Bomb

*Prep Time 5 minutes*

*Cook Time 10 minutes*

*Total Time 15 minutes*

*Serves 8*

*Ingredients*

10 drops vanilla stevia drops

1/4 cup coconut oil about

1/4 cup cocoa butter about

*Directions*

1. Melt the coconut oil and cocoa butter in a double boiler or in a skillet over low heat.

2. Remove from heat and stir in a few stevia drops. Pour the mixture into molds and keep it refrigerated until hardened or ready to serve.

3. To serve, remove from the molds and store any remainder in the fridge.

*Calories 125, Carbs 0g, Protein 0g, Fat 10g*

## Keto Macaroon Fat Bombs

*Prep Time: 15 minutes*

*Cook Time: 15 minutes*

*Total Time: 30 minutes*

*Serves: 10*

*Ingredients*

3 egg whites

1 tablespoon coconut oil

1 tablespoon vanilla extract

2 tablespoons Swerve

½ cup shredded coconut

1/4 cup almond flour

*Directions*

1. Mix coconut, almond flour and swerve in a bowl until well incorporated.

2. In a small saucepan, melt coconut oil; and then add in vanilla extract.

3. Meanwhile, keep a medium bowl in the refrigerator to be used for mounting the egg whites.

4. Add in melted coconut oil to the coconut almond flour mix and mix well.

5. Now place the egg whites in the chilled bowl and whisk continuously until hard or it becomes foamy with holding stiff peaks.

6. Slowly incorporate the egg whites into the flour mix, taking care not to over mix and preserve some of the egg whites.

7. Spoon the batter into muffin cups or onto a cookie sheet and bake at 400 degrees F until the macaroons begin to brown on tops. This should take around 8 minutes.

8. Remove from the oven and let them cool, then remove from the muffin cups and serve.

*Calories: 46, Carbs 1g, Protein: 1.8g, Fat: 5g*

## Keto Chocolate Pots de Crème

*Prep Time 10 minutes*

*Cook Time 1 hour*

*Total Time 1 hour 10 minutes*

*Serves 6*

*Ingredients*

4 egg yolks

Pinch salt

1 teaspoon vanilla extract

3 tablespoons erythritol

4 oz. dark chocolate baking chips

12 oz. heavy cream

*Directions*

1. Prepare a water bath at 80 degrees Celsius, or 176 degree F. Then bring the heavy cream to simmer in a saucepan.

2. Whisk in dark chocolate chips, salt, vanilla and erythritol and remove from heat once blended.

3. Whisk in egg yolks one by one until you get a smooth mixture. Move the mixture to a pourable measuring cup to help you distribute the mixture.

4. Distribute the mixture among six 4-ounce mason jars, then screw on lids tight. Put the sealed jars at the bottom of prepared water bath.

5. Cook the custards in the water bath for 1 hour, and then remove the sealed jars from water with tongs. Take care not to burn, as they are very hot!

6. Put the jars in your refrigerator to cool down and set for at least 3 hours.

7. Serve the chocolate pots de crème with cinnamon and whipped cream.

*Calories 309, Carbs 11g, Protein 4g, Fat 29g*

## Keto Chocolate Soufflé

*Prep Time 5 minutes*

*Cook Time 25 minutes*

*Total Time 30 minutes*

*Serves 4*

*Ingredients*

6 large egg whites

3 large egg yolks at room temperature

5 oz. unsweetened chocolate

⅓ cup Lakanto Monk Fruit sugar plus 2 tablespoons

1 tablespoon butter for buttering dish

Coconut whipped cream

*Directions*

1. Preheat your oven to 375 degrees F. Meanwhile grease or butter a soufflé dish and set it aside.

2. In a metal bowl that is set over simmering water, melt some unsweetened chocolate while stirring continuously until well melted.

3. Remove the melted chocolate from heat and whisk in egg yolks into the bowl. Whisk using a fork until the mixture has hardened.

4. Now in a separate bowl, whisk in egg whites along with some salt with an electric mixer at high speed while adding third cup of the sugar-free syrup a little by little. Whisk until stiff peaks appear.

5. Stir in 1 cup of the egg whites to the mixture and add in the rest of the egg whites, while folding the mixture thoroughly using a silicon spatula.

6. Pour the mixture into the prepared soufflé dish and now run the end of your thumb inside the edge of the dish to make the soufflé rise evenly.

7. Bake the chocolate batter in the preheated oven for 20 minutes or until puffed and crushed on top. Serve the soufflé while hot.

*Calories: 320, Carbs 3.4g, Protein 11g, Fat: 25g*

# Cakes

## Low Carb Slow Cooker Cheesecake

*Prep Time: 30 minutes*

*Cook Time: 4 hours 30 minutes*

*Total Time: 5 hours*

*Serves 8*

*Ingredients*

1/2 tablespoon vanilla

1 cup Splenda

3 eggs

3 (8 oz.) packages cream cheese

*Directions*

1. Let the cream cheese get to room temperature and put it in a large bowl. Add in a sweetener.

2. Using a mixer, combine cream cheese and the sweetener until well incorporated.

3. Add in eggs one by one, and mix to blend. Now coat the slow cooker bowl with cooking spray and then pour the cream cheese mixture.

4. Add a few cups of water to the slow cooker to last for 2 hours and then put the cheesecake into the cooking bowl.

5. Close the lid in place and cook on high heat for about two and two and a half hours.

6. If the mixture puffs during cooking don't worry, it will go down. Start checking the cheesecake after two hours. When a knife is inserted into the mixture, it should come out clean.

*Calories 317.1, Carbs 9.7g Protein 8.4g, Fat 31.0g*

## Crust-less Keto Cheesecake

*Prep Time: 15 minutes*

*Cook Time: 50 minutes*

*Total Time: 1 hour 5 minutes*

*Serves: 10*

*Ingredients*

4 eggs

⅓ cup sour cream

1 teaspoons vanilla

1 cup of sweetener

3 (8-oz.) packages of cream cheese

*Directions*

1. Preheat your oven to 350 degrees F. Beat cream cheese for about 3 minutes, or until fluffy.

2. Mix the cream cheese with the sweetener, vanilla extract and sour cream. Mix for around 3 minutes.

3. Beat in the eggs one at a time until thick and creamy.

4. Grease a 9-inch spring-form pan and place the pan on a baking sheet.

5. Pour in the filling and bake in the preheated oven until puffy and lightly brown on the edges. This should take 50-55 minutes.

6. Set on a wire rack to cool for 1-2 hours. Then cover, and keep frozen for about 4 hours.

*Calories 278, Carbs 3.31g, Protein 6.64 g, Fat 26.70g*

## Keto Dark Chocolate Cake

*Prep Time: 10 minutes*

*Cook Time: 3 hours*

*Total Time: 3 hours 10 minutes*

*Serves 10*

*Ingredients*

1/3 cup sugar-free chocolate chips

3/4 teaspoon vanilla extract

2/3 cup unsweetened almond milk

6 tablespoons butter, melted

3 large eggs

¼ teaspoon salt

1 1/2 teaspoons baking powder

3 tablespoons egg white protein powder, unflavored

1/2 cup cocoa powder

1/2 cup Swerve Granular

1 cup plus 2 tablespoons almond flour

*Directions*

1.  Grease a crockpot and set aside. Whisk together almond flour, salt, baking powder, protein powder, cocoa powder and the sweetener in a medium bowl.

2. Then stir in eggs, butter, vanilla extract and almond milk until well incorporated. Stir in chocolate if you like to include it.

3. Pour the batter into the crockpot's insert and cook for about 2 -2 ½ hours on low heat.

4. Once you achieve cake consistency, turn off the cooker and allow to cool for about 20 to 30 minutes.

5. Finally cut into pieces and serve it when hot or warm. Serve with unsweetened whipped cream.

*Calories 205, Carbs 8.42g Protein: 7.37g, Fat: 16.97g*

## Keto Chocolate Molten Lava Cake

*Prep Time: 10 minutes*

*Cook Time: 3 hours*

*Total Time: 3 hour 10 minutes*

*Serves 12*

*Ingredients*

2 cups hot water

4 ounce chocolate chips, sugar free

1/2 teaspoon vanilla liquid stevia

1 teaspoon vanilla extract

3 egg yolks

3 whole eggs

1/2 cup butter melted, cooled

1 teaspoon baking powder

1/2 teaspoon salt

5 tablespoons cocoa powder, unsweetened

1/2 cup almond flour

1 1/2 cups Swerve sweetener divided

*Directions*

## Keto Diet Desserts

1. Coat the slow cooker with oil. Whisk flour, baking powder, 3 tablespoons cocoa powder, almond flour and 1 1/4 cup Swerve in a bowl.

2. In a separate bowl, stir eggs with melted butter, liquid Stevia, vanilla extract, and egg yolks.

3. Add the wet ingredients to the dry ones and combine to fully incorporate. Pour the mixture in the slow cooker.

4. Top the mixture with chocolate chips. In a separate bowl, whisk together the remaining swerve with cocoa powder and hot water and pour this mixture over chocolate chips.

5. Pour the mixture into your slow cooker, cover and cook on low for around 3 hours. Once done, let it cool and then serve.

*Calories 157, Carbs 10.5g, Protein 3.9g, Fat 13g*

# Blueberry Lemon Custard Cake

*Prep Time: 15 minutes*

*Cook Time: 3 hours*

*Total Time: 3 hours 15 minutes*

*Serves 12*

*Ingredients*

1/2 cup fresh blueberries

2 cups heavy cream

1/2 teaspoon salt

1/2 cup Swerve sweetener

1 teaspoon lemon liquid stevia

1/3 cup lemon juice

2 teaspoons lemon zest

1/2 cup coconut flour

6 eggs separated

*Directions*

1. Put egg whites in a stand mixture and whip to achieve stiff peaks consistency.

2. Set the egg whites aside then whisk the yolks along with the other ingredients apart from the blueberries.

## Keto Diet Desserts

3. Fold the egg whites into the batter to fully combine, and then grease the slow cooker.

4. Now pour the mixture into the pot and top with the blue berries. Cover the crockpot and cook on low for about 3 hours. (When cooked through, a toothpick inserted in the cake should come out clean).

5. Let cool while not covered for 1 hour then keep it chilled for at least 2 hours or overnight.

6. Serve the cake topped with unsweetened cream if you like.

*Calories 191, Carbs 4g, Protein 4g, Fat 17g*

# Almond Sponge Cake with Lemon Curd

*Prep Time: 15 minutes*

*Cook Time: 40 minutes*

*Total Time: 55 minutes*

*Serves 4 (approx. 8 to 9 inch cake)*

Ingredients

1 3/4 cups almond flour

Zest of one lemon

1 tablespoon vanilla, alcohol-free

4 packets Stevia

1/2 cup plain yogurt

5 egg yolks

5 egg whites

*For the lemon curd*

2 tablespoons lemon juice

1/4 cup coconut oil, melted

Zest of one lemon, organic

1 teaspoon alcohol free vanilla

3 packets of stevia

3 eggs

*Directions*

1. Prepare the curd by whisking together lemon zest, alcohol free vanilla, stevia and eggs in a medium bowl. Add in melted coconut oil and continue to whisk to blend. Once fully incorporated whisk in lemon juice.

2. Put a pan with the contents over medium heat while whisking continuously, until the mixture is opaque. After about 1-2 minutes, the mixture should start to thicken.

3. Remove the pan from the heat and transfer the curd into a bowl, if need be using a mesh strainer. Now start to prepare the cake by brushing coconut or olive oil onto the sides and bottom of an 8 or 9-inch pan.

4. Cut out a parchment paper that fits the bottom of your cake jar, place in pan and brush with additional oil. Set it aside.

5. Beat egg whites in a medium bowl until stiff peaks form and set the eggs aside. Then whisk lemon zest, alcohol free vanilla, stevia, yoghurt and egg yolks in a small bowl and set aside.

6. Next, add the egg yolk mixture, egg whites and almond flour into a large bowl and fold gently to blend. Pour this mixture in a prepared pan and bake the contents for 20-25 minutes.

7. When done, the top of the cakes should spring back when pressed. Likewise, a toothpick inserted in the center should come out clean.

8. Now cool for 10 minutes while still inside the pan, and then run a knife around the edge of the pan in order to loosen the cake. To remove the cake from the pan, invert the cake and then remove the parchment paper.

9. Re-invert the cake and then transfer to a wire rack to fully cool. Slice using a serrated knife and then serve with lemon curd.

*Calories 345, Carbs 7.7g, Proteins 15.8g, Fat 27.9g*

# Almond flour Mocha Fudge Cake

*Prep Time: 15 minutes*

*Cook Time: 2 hours*

*Total Time: 2 hours 15 minutes*

*Serves: as required*

*Ingredients*

1/2 teaspoon Celtic sea salt

1 1/2 teaspoon vanilla or chocolate extract

3/4 cup hot coffee

1 1/2 teaspoon baking soda

1 1/2 cups blanched almond flour

3/4 cup sour cream

3 oz. unsweetened chocolate, melted

3 eggs

4 tablespoons butter or coconut oil

1 1/2 cups Swerve

*Directions*

1. Grease the crockpot with oil. Beat coconut oil and natural sweetener in a bowl until fully incorporated.

2. Beat in eggs, cream and chocolate. In a bowl, sift baking soda and almond flour and add in the chocolate mixture.

3. Beat in coffee, salt and vanilla until well incorporated. Once done, pour the batter into the cooking pot of the slow cooker.

4. Cook on low for 2 to 4 hours or until a toothpick inserted in the cake comes out clean.

*Calories 200, Carbs 5.8g, Protein 6g, Fat 18g*

# Instant Pot Brownie Cake

*Prep Time: 10 minutes*

*Cook Time: 18 minutes*

*Total Time: 28 minutes*

*Serves: 4*

*Ingredients*

4 tablespoons cocoa powder, unsweetened

½ cup coconut or almond flour

¼ teaspoon vanilla extract

2 Eggs

2/3 cup erythritol

2 tablespoons chocolate chips

4 tablespoons unsalted butter

*Directions*

1. Microwave chocolate chips and butter in a microwave-safe bowl for a minute.

2. Once melted, beat the chocolate chips, sugar and butter in a mixing bowl until well incorporated.

3. Add in vanilla and egg, and beat to mix. Then add in cocoa and flour over the wet ingredients and mix until blended.

4. Put the rack inside the cooking pot and add a cup of water in the bottom of Instant Pot.

5. Add batter to ramekins and put them on the rack inside the pot. Use aluminum foil to cover the tops.

6. Cook for 18 minutes on high pressure, then quick release pressure. Serve.

*Calories 156, Carbs 5.1g, Protein 6g, Fat 13g*

## Crock Pot Fudge

*Prep Time: 5 minutes*

*Cook Time: 2 hours*

*Total Time: 2 hours 5 minutes*

*Serves 30*

*Ingredients*

A dash of salt

1 teaspoon vanilla extract

1/3 cup coconut milk

2 1/2 cups sugar-free chocolate chips

2 teaspoons vanilla liquid stevia

*Directions*

1. In a slow cooker pot, stir in coconut milk, stevia, vanilla, chocolate chips and salt.

2. Cover the crockpot and cook on low for about 2 hours. Once done cooking, uncover and let it sit for about 30 minutes undisturbed.

3. Then stir well for about 5 minutes or until smooth. Using parchment paper line a casserole dish and then spread the mixture in.

4. Keep refrigerated until firm, or for around 30 minutes or so.

*Calories 65, Carbs 2g, Protein 1g, Fat 5g*

# Almond and Coconut Muffin

*Prep Time: 3 minutes*

*Cook Time: 1 minute*

*Total Time: 4 minutes*

*Serves 1*

*Ingredients*

1 teaspoon extra virgin olive oil

1 large egg

1/8 teaspoon salt

1/4 teaspoon baking powder

1/2 teaspoon cinnamon

1 teaspoon sucralose based sweetener

1/3 tablespoon organic coconut flour

2 tablespoons almond meal flour

*Directions*

1. Add all the ingredients in a coffee mug and stir to incorporate.

2. Add in oil and egg, and mix well.

3. Microwave for about 60 seconds then remove the muffin from the cup using a knife.

4. Slice, apply butter and serve.

*Calories 208.5, Carbs 3.4g, Protein 9.7g, Fat 16.8g*

# Bread and Pies

## Almond Flour Goji Buns

*Prep Time: 20 minutes*

*Cook Time: 20 minutes*

*Total Time: 40 minutes*

*Serves 10*

*Ingredients*

1 tablespoon Stevia powder, sweetener

2 tablespoons cooking cream, about 35% fat

Pinch of salt

1 teaspoon baking powder

1 tablespoon flaxseed, ground

2 tablespoons goji berries, dried and ground

3 tablespoons almond flour, preferably Bob's Red Mill

5 tablespoons coconut oil

4 eggs, whole

30g salted butter

*Directions*

1. Preheat your oven to 350 degrees F.

2. Using an electric mixer, beat eggs well in a medium sized or large bowl. Then blend oil into the eggs, gradually adding a tablespoon and continue to whisk.

3. Once done, blend the cream into the mixture, adding a tablespoon at a time as you whisk until fully incorporated.

4. Add in some warm melted butter into the mixture, and combine with the rest of the ingredients fully, before adding the liquid sweetener.

5. Add in the mixed dry ingredients comprising of salt, baking powder, flaxseed, goji beans and almond flour to the cream batter. You just need to add a tablespoon at each time, as you gently mix by hand.

6. Once done, transfer the dough to a non-stick cup bun tray.

7. Bake for around 15 minutes, up until the buns' tops turn golden. After removing the baked buns from the oven, they will deflate slightly.

8. Serve the cups when hot, and then store the remaining cups in the fridge.

*Calories 145, Carbs 2.6g, Proteins 3.2g, Fat 13.6g*

# Sugar-free Mud Pie

*Prep Time: 20 minutes*

*Cook Time: 40 minutes*

*Total Time: 1 hour*

*Serves 10*

*Ingredients*

*Sugar-free gummy worms*

1/2 cup water

2-4g packets gelatin

2-8g packets sugar-free Jell-O

*For Cake Base*

1/4 cup almond milk

1/2 cup heavy cream

2 teaspoon vanilla extract

3 large eggs

1 cup melted butter

1/2 teaspoon salt

1.5 teaspoon baking soda

1 cup erythritol

1/2 cup cocoa powder (sifted)

2 tablespoons coconut flour

2 cups almond flour

*For frosting*

2 tablespoons almond milk

1/2 cup powdered erythritol

1.5 tablespoon cocoa powder

1/4 cup butter

*Directions*

1. Start making gummy worms the night before. Just whisk together the gelatin, Jell-O and a 1/4 cup of water in a small pot over low heat.

2. As soon as the clumps of the gelatin disappears, pour the liquids into molds.

3. Keep it refrigerated preferably overnight.

4. To make the cake base, preheat the oven to 350 degrees F and whisk the dry ingredients: salt, baking soda, erythritol, almond flour and coconut flour.

5. Add in the wet ingredients; almond milk, heavy cream, vanilla extract, eggs and melted butter.

6. Grease a 9*9 inch baking pan with butter or oil and then pour the batter. Bake for around 35-40 minutes and once ready, allow it to cool completely.

7. To make the frosting, melt butter in a saucepan. Once it has melted, turn off the heat and then stir in almond milk, powdered erythritol and cocoa powder.

8. Once the cake is cooled, crumble it using your hands. Pour in the frosting and mix.

9. Press the cake into a 9 by 10 inch spring form, and then layer with the gummy worms you made followed by more cake crumbs until you reach the top.

10. Lastly, add some chocolate chips and freeze for 2-4 hours.

*Calories400, Carbs 4g, Protein 7g, Fat 40g*

## **Blackberry Clafouti**

*Prep Time: 10 Minutes*

*Cook Time: 45 Minutes*

*Total Time: 55 minutes*

*Serves 8*

*Ingredients*

1/3 cup xylitol

1 cup heavy cream

4 large egg (whole)

1/2 teaspoon cinnamon

1/4 teaspoon salt

1 teaspoon vanilla extract

0.375 cup almond meal flour

1/2 teaspoon pure almond extract

1/4 cup unsalted butter stick

6 oz. blackberries

1 pinch Stevia

1 teaspoon lemon zest

*Directions*

1. Preheat the oven to 325 degrees F. Meanwhile grease a baking dish with butter.

2. Layer the blackberries on the shallow baking dish and set aside.

3. Now whisk together eggs, almond flour, salt and granular sugar substitute.

4. Add in cinnamon, lemon zest, almond extract, vanilla, melted butter and cream then whisk to mix.

5. Pour the mixture over the reserved blackberries and bake until puffed and set in the center, or for around 30 to 45 minutes.

6. Cool the clafouti for 20 minutes then serve it warm. You can keep refrigerated for 3 days.

*Calories 252.3, Carbs 2.3g, Protein 5.2g, Fat 22g*

## Strawberry Cream Pie

*Prep Time: 30 minutes*

*Chill Time: 3 hours*

*Total Time: 30 minutes*

*Serves: 10*

*Ingredients*

*Shortbread Crust:*

1/4 cup butter melted

1/4 teaspoon salt

1/4 cup Swerve Sweetener, powdered

1 1/2 cups almond flour

*Strawberry Cream Filling:*

3/4 teaspoon vanilla extract

1/2 cup powdered Swerve Sweetener

1 cup heavy whipping cream

2 1/2 teaspoons grass-fed gelatin

1/4 cup water

1 1/2 cups chopped fresh strawberries

Extra whipped cream for serving

## Keto Diet Desserts

*Directions*

1. To make the shortbread crust, whisk together the sweetener, almond flour and salt in a medium bowl.

2. Add in the melted butter and continue to whisk until the dough comes together and looks like coarse crumbs.

3. Move the crumbs into a ceramic or glass pie plate and firmly press into the bottom and the sides. Use a measuring cup or flat-bottomed glass to even out the bottom.

4. Keep the mixture frozen as you make the filling. To make the strawberry cream filling, first puree strawberries and water in food processor or blender.

5. Move the strawberry mixture to a saucepan and whisk in gelatin. Over medium low heat, bring the contents to a simmer, while you whisk to blend in the gelatin. Allow to cook for about 20 minutes.

6. Mix together vanilla extract, sweetener, and the cream in a large bowl, and beat this mixture until you get stiff peaks.

7. Spoon the mixture in the crust you have prepared and keep it frozen for about 4 hours.

8. Serve the pie garnished with fresh berries and whipped cream.

*Calories 233, Carbs 6.2g, Protein 4.8g, Fat 21.1g*

# Pecan Pie

*Prep Time: 25 minutes*

*Cook Time: 1 hour 5 minutes*

*Total Time: 3 hours 30 minutes*

*Yields: 10 slices*

*Ingredients*

*Crust*

1/2 teaspoon pink salt

3/4 teaspoon vanilla extract

3/4 tablespoon coconut oil

6 tablespoons butter

3 tablespoons erythritol

1.5 large eggs

3/4 cup coconut flour

*Filling*

1 1/2 cups raw pecans roughly chopped

1 teaspoon vanilla extract

10 tablespoons sugar free maple syrup

2 tablespoons butter

10 tablespoons erythritol

2 large eggs

*Directions*

1. Begin by making the crust. In a bowl, mix all the dry ingredients and then mix together all the wet ingredients in a separate bowl.

2. Once well mixed, begin to add in the dry mixture into the wet ingredients. Stir the until well combined to form soft dough.

3. Now grease a pie pan and then press the dough into the bottom and the sides of your pan.

4. Bake the crust dough in a preheated oven at 350 degrees F for 12 to 15 minutes. Check on the crust edges to ensure that it doesn't burn!

5. Once cooked through, remove from the oven and allow to cool until easier to handle, or store it overnight in your fridge.

6. Start preparing the filing by adding together all the ingredients in a mixing bowl apart from pecans. Mix well.

7. Layer the bottom of the cooled crust using one-and a half cups of the pecans. Pour the wet filling mixture over the pecans fully covering them.

8. Put the pie in a 350 degrees hot oven and bake for approximately 50 minutes.

9. Remove from the oven and let it cool for a few hours before serving. Slice it up and enjoy it at room temperature, or instead reheat it.

*Calories 259.2, Carbs 9.3g, Protein 4.65g, Fat 25g*

# Keto Pistachio Pudding Pie

*Prep Time: 20 minutes*

*Cook Time: 12 minutes*

*Total Time: 32 minutes*

*Serves: 12 servings*

*Ingredients*

*For the pie crust:*

1 batch Keto pistachio shortbread cookie dough

Filling

1/2 teaspoon vanilla extract

2 tablespoons powdered erythritol

2 packages pistachio pudding mix, sugar free

1.5 cups unsweetened almond milk

1.5 cups heavy whipping cream

8 ounces mascarpone cheese

3 tablespoons pistachios for garnish

*Directions*

1. To make the bread crust, first preheat the oven to 350 degrees. Meanwhile, start preparing the filling by mixing together almond milk, ½ cup whipping cream and

mascarpone along with pistachio pudding mix in a large bowl.

2. Stir together the ingredients and keep chilled for around 15 minutes.

3. Press the pistachio cookie dough firmly in a medium-sized pie plate and bake the dough for about 12 minutes.

4. Once cooked through, remove from the oven and let it cool. Back to the filling, as it cools, mix together vanilla extract, 1 cup whipping cream and erythritol in a large mixing bowl.

5. Beat the mixture using an electric mixer or a whisk until you obtain stiff peaks. Then fold half of the cream mixture gently over the chilled filling (pistachio almond milk mixture).

6. Spoon the pistachio almond mixture into the cooked pie and smooth out evenly. Either serve it at room temperature or chill for some time.

7. If you like it, you can garnish with chopped pistachios

*Calories: 402, Fat: 37g, Carbs: 8g, Protein: 6g*

# Easy & Delicious Keto Pie

*Prep Time 10 minutes*

*Cook Time 10 minutes*

*Total Time 25 minutes*

*Servings: 8*

*Ingredients*

*For the Crust:*

1 teaspoon Swerve granulated

2 tablespoon butter, melted

1 cup chopped pecans

*For the Pie Filling:*

1 teaspoon vanilla extract

2/3 cup Swerve confectioners

1 cup strawberries, chopped

1 1/2 cups heavy whipping cream

8 oz. Philadelphia Cream Cheese, softened

*Directions*

1. Begin by making the crust. Preheat the oven to 350 degree F and then finely crush the pecans.

2. To the crushed pecans, add in butter and swerve and mix them thoroughly. You can alternatively add the mixture to a mini processor and pulse until fully combined.

3. Grease a pie pan and add in the crust mixture. Spoon the pecan mixture in the bottom and up the sides of the baking pan using the back of a greased spoon.

4. Bake for about 10 minutes and then cool as you prepare the filling. Now in a bowl, beat together heavy whipping cream until you have stiff peaks.

5. Add vanilla, softened cream cheese, swerve and a cup of chopped strawberries in a bowl and beat on medium speed to get a smooth mixture. Mix until the strawberries start to break down and make the filling pink.

6. Add in the whipping cream and beat until smooth. Pour the filling mixture into the pecan pie crust and keep it chilled for about 1 to 2 hours to set up.

7. Serve and enjoy. You can also store the pie in the fridge for 1 to 2 hours and then serve.

*Calories 377, Carbs 5g, Protein 3g, Fat 38g*

# Dream Pie

*Prep Time 10 minutes*

*Cook Time 10 minutes*

*Total Time 20 minutes*

*Servings 8*

## Ingredients

*Crust*

1/4 teaspoon stevia extract powder

3 tablespoons butter, melted

2 cups flaked coconut, unsweetened

*Filling*

2 teaspoons sugar-free vanilla extract

2 cups heavy cream, chilled

1/2 cup cocoa powder

1/4 teaspoon stevia concentrated powder

2/3 cups powdered erythritol

1/4 cup boiling water

2 tablespoons cold water

1 tablespoon grass-fed gelatin

## Keto Diet Desserts

*Directions*

1. To a bowl, add in melted butter and Stevia to flaked coconut. Press the mixture in a pie plate and bake the mixture at 325 degrees F or until the coconut is golden brown.

2. Sprinkle gelatin over cold water in a small bowl, and allow to stand for about 1 minute or so.

3. Add in boiling water and stir until the gelatin is fully dissolved and the mixture turns clear. Cool for some time.

4. Stir together cocoa and the sweetener in a medium bowl, and add in vanilla and whipping cream.

5. Beat the contents using an electric mixer on medium speed, while scrapping the bottom of the bowl and again, until you get stiff peaks,

6. Pour in the dissolved gelatin mixture and beat to blend. Spoon the mixture into the pie crust.

*Calories 354, Carbs 7g, Protein 4g, Fat 29g*

# Keto Cream Pie

*Prep Time 20 minutes*

*Cook Time 18 minutes*

*Total Time 1 hour 8 minutes*

*Serves*

*Ingredients*

*Base*

2 oz. butter, melted

2 tablespoons truvia

1/4 cup cocoa powder

1/2 cup almond meal

Filling

1/2 cup sugar free chocolate chips

1 teaspoon vanilla extract

1/4 cup water boiling

0.3 oz. sugar free jello raspberry

2 tablespoons truvia

2/3 cup heavy cream

8 oz. cream cheese softened

*Topping*

1 cup heavy cream whipped

*Directions*

1. Begin with the cake base. Preheat the oven to 320 degrees F and then mix butter, cocoa powder, truvia and almond meal in a bowl.

2. Press the cocoa almond mixture into a pie plate and bake until firm around the edges, or for about 18 minutes. Once slightly puffed in the middle, let the cake base cool

3. Start making the filling. First, dissolve the jello in boiling water and let it cool for some time.

4. To the bowl of your stand mixer, add in vanilla extract, truvia, heavy cream and the softened cream cheese. Whip the mixture on medium speed until well blended.

5. Set the stand mixer to low speed and slowly pour in the jello mixture into the cheese mixture. Turn the speed to medium speed and now whip until the mixture is incorporated.

6. Remove the bowl from the stand mixer and then fold in the chocolate chips through the cream cheese and jello mixture.

7. Pour the mixture on the cooled chocolate crust and spread it in an even layer. Put into your refrigerator for around 30 minutes or so.

8. Once set, top the cream pie with fresh whipped heavy cream. Cut the pie into 12 pieces and enjoy.

*Calories 245, Carbs 4g, Protein 3g, Fat 25g*

# Brownies and Cookies

## Nut Free Keto Brownie

*Prep Time 10 minutes*

*Cook Time 20 minutes*

*Total Time 30 minutes*

*Servings 12*

*Ingredients*

120g cream cheese softened

3 - 5 tablespoons granulated sweetener

2 teaspoons vanilla

1/2 teaspoon baking powder

60g cocoa unsweetened

160g butter, melted

6 eggs

*Directions*

1. To a mixing bowl, add in all the ingredients and then blend until smooth using a stick blender that has a blade attachment.

2. Pour the batter into a 21 by 8.5 inch baking dish. Bake at 350 degrees F until well cooked at the center. This takes 20-25 minutes.

3. Slice the brownie into squares, triangle wedges or rectangle bars and serve.

*Calories 178, Carbs 3.5g, Protein 4.5g, Fat 17g*

## Keto Avocado Brownies

*Prep Time 10 minutes*

*Cook Time 35 minutes*

*Total Time 45 minutes*

*Yields 12 squares*

*Ingredients*

100g chocolate chips melted

2 eggs

3 tablespoons lard, shortening, ghee, butter or unrefined coconut oil

1 teaspoon monk fruit powder or stevia powder

4 tablespoons cocoa powder

1/2 teaspoon vanilla

250 g avocado

*Dry Ingredients*

60 ml erythritol or xylitol

1/4 teaspoon salt

1 teaspoon baking powder

1/4 teaspoon baking soda

90g blanched almond flour (10 tablespoon tightly packed)

*Directions*

1. Preheat the oven to 350 degrees F. Meanwhile peel the avocados and put them in a blender or food processor.

2. Add in all the ingredients to the food processor but one at a time and puree for a few seconds until you have added all the ingredients part from the dry ones.

3. Mix all the dry ingredients in a separate bowl and whisk them together. Add the mixture to the food processor and blend well.

4. Put a piece of a parchment paper over a 12 by 8 inch baking dish and then put in the batter.

5. Place in the preheated oven and bake for about 35 minutes. Remove from the oven, allow to cool and then slice the brownie.

*Calories 158, Carbs 9.01g, Protein 3.84g, Fat 14.29g*

## Keto Peanut Butter Cookies

*Prep Time 10 minutes*

*Cook Time 15 minutes*

*Total Time 25 minutes*

*Serves 15*

*Ingredients*

1 cup peanut butter, plain butter

1 large egg

1/2 cup Stevia or erythritol, or monk fruit

*Directions*

1. Preheat your oven to 350 degrees F. Add all the ingredients into a medium size bowl and mix them until incorporated.

2. Roll the dough formed into approximately 1-inch balls with your hands or using a scoop.

3. Put the balls on a cookie sheet that is lined with silicone baking mat or parchment paper. Silicone baking mats are preferable in that they produce evenly cooked cookies with a crust that comes out perfectly.

4. Using a fork, press down on each individual ball twice in opposite direction to create a crisscross pattern.

5. Bake the cookies until golden brown or for around 12 to 15 minutes. Let them cool for approximately 5 minutes and then remove them from the tray.

6. Keep the cookies in an airtight container and serve them as required.

*Calories 108, Carbs 4.7g, Protein 4.2g, Fat 9.2g*

## Keto Fudgy Brownie Cookies

*Prep Time: 5 minutes*

*Cook Time: 13 minutes*

*Total Time: 18 minutes*

*Yields: 10 cookies*

*Ingredients*

1/2 cup sugar free chocolate chips

1 teaspoon vanilla extract

1 pinch salt

1 teaspoon baking soda

1/2 cup cocoa powder

2 eggs beaten

3/4 cup xylitol

1/3 cup coconut flour

3/4 cup butter melted

*Directions*

1. Preheat the oven to 350 degrees F. Meanwhile line your baking sheet with a parchment paper.

2. Mix xylitol, coconut flour and melted butter in a large bowl, and then add in beaten eggs.

3. Beat the mixture using a whisk or an electric beater, until well blended. Add in salt, vanilla extract, baking soda and cocoa powder. Beat again to mix.

4. Pour in chocolate chips and mix using a rubber spatula, to create a very thick batter.

5. Scoop out about 10 cookies with a large cookie scoop onto the prepared baking sheet. Press a couple of chocolate chips say around 3 to 4 on top of the cookies.

6. Move the cookies to the preheated oven and bake for approximately 13 minutes or so.

7. Once cooked through, remove from the oven and allow to cool fully before you serve these yummy brownie cookies.

*Calories 208, carbs 3.7g, Protein 3.7g, Fat 20g*

# Almond Butter Brownie Cookies

*Prep Time 5 minutes*

*Cook Time 10 minutes*

*Total Time 15 minutes*

*Yields: 14*

*Ingredients*

3 tablespoons unsweetened almond milk

1 large egg

1/4 cup chocolate chips, sugar free

1/2 cup granulated erythritol or monk fruit

4 tablespoons unsweetened cocoa powder

1 cup almond butter smooth

*Directions*

1. Preheat the oven to 350 degrees F.

2. Combine the sweetener, cocoa powder, egg and almond butter in a medium bowl. Mix with a fork until well incorporated.

3. In case the mixture appears crumbly, add 3 tablespoons of almond milk to thin a little. Ensure you have a fudgy and soft batter, and not runny.

4. Roll the balls manually with your hands and then press the balls down on a baking pan that is lined with parchment paper.

5. Bake the cookies until the tops start to show some cracks, or for about 10 to 12 minutes.

6. Allow the cookies to cool fully before serving.

*Calories 141, Carbs 2.9g, Protein 5.5g, Fat 12.1g*

## No Bake Brownie Cookies

*Prep Time 5 minutes*

*Cook Time 5 minutes*

*Total Time 10 minutes*

*Yields 20 Cookies*

Ingredients

1/4 cup stevia sweetened chocolate chips

3/4 cup coconut flour

1/2 cup monk fruit sweetened maple syrup

2 cups chocolate spread of choice

*Directions*

1. Melt the chocolate spread on a stove top or microwave-safe bowl along with monk fruit sweetened maple syrup until well mixed.

2. Add in flour and mix well to get thick dough. Add in some chocolate chips to the dough.

3. Roll the dough into small balls using your hands and put them on a parchment lined plate.

4. Press each individual ball into a cookie shape, and once done keep all the balls frozen in an air-tight container to firm up.

*Keto Diet Desserts*

*Calories 97, Carbs 2g, Protein 4.5g, Fat 7.5g*

# Skillet Brownies

*Prep Time 15 minutes*

*Cook Time 30 minutes*

*Serves 4*

*Ingredients*

1/4 cup walnuts

1/2 teaspoon baking powder

1/4 cup almond flour

1 pinch salt

1/2 teaspoon vanilla extract

1 egg

1/3 cup cocoa powder

1/3 cup erythritol

6 tablespoon butter

*Peanut Butter Drizzle*

1 tablespoon butter

1 tablespoon peanut butter

*Directions*

## Keto Diet Desserts

1. Preheat your oven to 350 degrees F. Meanwhile melt some butter in a small pan over medium heat.

2. Allow the granulated sweetener of choice such as erythritol to dissolve in the hot butter for approximately 5 minutes or so.

3. Pour the hot butter along with dissolved erythritol into a bowl and add in vanilla extract, salt and cocoa powder.

4. Add in the egg and beat the mixture until fully incorporated. To the smooth mixture, add in baking powder and almond flour.

5. If you like, fold in a few nuts such as chopped walnuts. Then pour the brownie batter into a cast iron skillet.

6. If you want, you can make peanut butter drizzle; simply melt butter along with peanut butter in a small pan or in your microwave. You can bake the brownie with the drizzle or alternatively add it later after baking.

7. Put the skillet brownie in the preheated oven and cook until the top is set but somehow jiggly, or for approximately 30 minutes.

8. You can add peanut butter drizzle and then top with sugar-free chocolate syrup or whipped cream.

*Calories 333, Carbs 3g, Protein 6g, Fat 31g*

## Collagen Protein Brownies

*Prep Time 10 minutes*

*Cook Time 20 minutes*

*Total Time 30 minutes*

*Serves 16*

*Ingredients*

2 teaspoons vanilla extract

2 oz. dark chocolate chips

1/4 cup almond milk, unsweetened

1/2 cup (4 large) egg whites

1/2 cup creamy almond butter

1/2 teaspoon salt

1/2 teaspoon baking soda

3/4 cup almond flour

1/2 cup cocoa powder, unsweetened

3/4 cup stevia-erythritol blend

120g collagen peptides, unflavored

*Directions*

1. Preheat your oven to 350 degrees F.

2. Meanwhile in a small mixing bowl whisk together all the dry ingredients and then add in all the wet ingredients. Combine well to mix.

3. Stir in the chocolate chips and set aside. Line your baking sheet with parchment paper and then use a spatula to spread the batter over the lined bottom.

4. Bake the batter until a toothpick inserted inside comes out somehow dirty or for approximately 18 to 20 minutes.

5. Allow to cool down for about 20 minutes and then cut into 8 pieces. Store any leftovers for up to a week in the refrigerator.

*Calories 130, Carbs: 5g, Protein: 11g, Fat: 8.4g*

## Chocolate Keto Brownies

*Prep Time: 20 minutes*

*Cook Time: 30 minutes*

*Total Time: 50 minutes*

*Serves 10*

*Ingredients*

1/2 teaspoon vanilla

1/4 teaspoon Himalayan pink salt

1/2 teaspoon baking soda

2 tablespoons collagen powder

1/2 cup cacao powder

1/2 cup coconut flour

1/4 cup erythritol

2 pasture-raised eggs

1 cup of avocado (about 2 medium fruits)

2 tablespoons grass-fed butter

3 oz. dark chocolate 85% or above

*Directions*

## Keto Diet Desserts

1. Preheat your oven to 350 degrees F. Meanwhile using parchment paper, line a 9 by 9 inch baking pan and set aside.

2. Over low heat, mix butter and dark chocolate in a small saucepan until well melted.

3. Now add the rest of the ingredients into a food processor beginning with the avocado and mix them well.

4. Add in butter and melted chocolate to the food processor and process the mixture until smooth, or for a minute or so.

5. Spread the thick gooey batter evenly on a prepared baking pan. Bake the brownie batter for approximately 25 minutes.

6. Insert a toothpick in the center of the brownie to check if it comes out clean, an indication of doneness. Then cool for a few minutes and slice into 10 equal pieces.

*Calories: 168.9, Carbs: 11g, Protein: 5.4g, Fat: 13.1g*

# Flourless Keto Brownies

*Prep Time 10 minutes*

*Cook Time 25 minutes*

*Total Time 35 minutes*

*Servings 16*

*Ingredients*

3 large eggs

1 additional egg or 1 tablespoon whole psyllium husks

1/4 cup unsweetened cocoa

2 teaspoons vanilla extract

1 1/4 teaspoon monk fruit liquid extract

1 1/4 teaspoon Sweetleaf stevia drops

8 ounces baking chocolate, unsweetened

1/4 teaspoon sea salt

1/2 cup coconut oil

*Directions*

1. Add the baking chocolate and coconut oil in a microwave-safe bowl and microwave until melted.

2. Add in vanilla extract, monk fruit, stevia and eggs to the melted chocolate and coconut oil mixture. Use an electric mixer to mix.

3. Stir in psyllium husks, cocoa and sea salt.

4. Spread the dough on an 8 by 8 inch baking pan that is lined with parchment paper.

5. Bake the brownies in the preheated oven for about 25 minutes, and then cool and slice the dessert.

*Calories 140, Carbs 5g, Protein 3.3g, Fat 15.3g*

# Custards and Puddings

## Keto Chocolate Mousse

*Prep Time: 15 minutes*

*Cook Time: 5 minutes*

*Total Time: 20 minutes*

*Serves: 8*

*Ingredients*

¼ cup heavy whipping cream

2-3 tablespoons Swerve sweetener

⅛ teaspoon vanilla extract

½ large avocado, pitted

¼ cup cocoa powder, unsweetened

8 ounces cream cheese block, softened

90% dark chocolate shaved, optional

*Directions*

1. Using a handheld mixer, beat cream cheese in a medium mixing bowl until smooth and creamy.

2. Mix in cocoa powder and beat in avocado. Continue to mix until fully incorporated, in about 5 minutes.

3. Add in the sweetener and vanilla extract and beat for 1-2 minutes, or until smooth.

4. Whip heavy cream into a bowl until stiff peaks form. Put the whipped cream in the chocolate mixture and gently fold to blend.

5. Put the chocolate mousse in a piping bag and pipe into various containers. If desired, garnish with dark chocolate shavings.

*Calories: 192, Carbs: 4.2g Protein: 2.4g, Fat: 11.1g*

# Almond Chia Seed Pudding

*Prep Time: 10 minutes*

*Cook Time: 1 hour*

*Total Time: 1 hour 19 minutes*

*Servings: 4*

*Ingredients*

2 tablespoons crushed roasted almonds

1/3 cup chia seeds

1 teaspoon pure vanilla extract

1/4 cup powered erythritol

1/4 cup cocoa powder, unsweetened

1/2 cup unsweetened coconut flakes, divided

2 cups unsweetened coconut milk

1/4 cup sugar-free dark chocolate chips optional

*Directions*

1. Mix vanilla extract, erythritol, cocoa powder, 1/4 cup of the coconut flakes and almond or coconut milk in a bowl. Combine the ingredients until well mixed.

2. Pour the incorporated mixture into a large mixing bowl and then add in the chia seeds. Whisk the mixture for about 1 or 2 minutes to fully combine.

3. Transfer the pudding into 4 serving cups or bowls and keep the pudding chilled for approximately 1 to 2 hours.

4. Top the pudding with almonds, chocolate chips and the reserved 1/4 cup of coconut flakes.

*Calories 125, Carbs 4.6g, Proteins 3.8g, Fat 16.4g*

## Keto Vanilla Custard

*Prep Time 10 minutes*

*Cook Time 10 minutes*

*Total Time 20 minutes*

*Serves 4*

*Ingredients*

¼ cup melted coconut oil

1 teaspoon (4 g) erythritol

1 teaspoon vanilla extract

½ cup almond milk, unsweetened

6 egg yolks

*Directions*

1. Whisk egg yolks, vanilla, sweetener and almond milk in a metal bowl.

2. Mix in coconut oil and put the metal bowl over a saucepan that has simmering water.

3. Whisk the ingredients until the mixture has thickened, for approximately 5 minutes.

4. As soon as the custard can coat the back of a spoon, remove from the water bath and serve it.

*Calories 215, Carbs 1g, Protein 4g, Fat 21g*

# Keto Baked Custard

*Prep Time 10 minutes*

*Cook Time 30 minutes*

*Total Time 40 minutes*

*Serves 4*

*Ingredients*

1/2 teaspoon ground cinnamon

1 teaspoon vanilla

1/4 cup stevia

1 cup cream

1 cup dairy-free milk

3 eggs

*Directions*

1. Preheat the oven to 350 degrees F in a heat-safe dish.

2. Whisk together all the ingredients in a large bowl until well incorporated.

3. Pour the batter into a parchment lined heat-safe dish and bake for approximately 30 minutes.

4. Once cooked through remove from the oven, cool and then serve either warm or cooled.

*Calories 177, Carbs 3g, Protein 8g, Fat 18g*

# Low Carb Custard Lemon

*Cook Time: 15 minutes*

*Chill time 2 hours*

*Total Time: 2 hours 15 minutes*

*Servings: 2*

*Ingredients*

1/8 teaspoon xanthan gum

15 drops liquid stevia

1/2 juice lemon

1 teaspoon lemon zest

4 large egg yolks

2 oz. cream cheese

4 tablespoons butter

*Directions*

1. Add cream cheese and butter to a saucepan over low heat, and let this melt.

2. Meanwhile grate in lemon zest, juice of half lemon and liquid Stevia and stir until well blended.

3. Add in an egg yolk one at a time as you whisk, to get a smooth and creamy mixture.

4. Cook the mixture for a few minutes and then add in xanthan gum. Mix well.

5. Remove from heat and transfer the mixture to a separate bowl. Cover with plastic wrap and keep in the fridge until set, or for about 2 hours.

*Calories 412, Carbs 3g, Protein 7g, Fat 41g*

# Keto Custard

*Prep Time 10 Minutes*

*Cook Time 30 Minutes*

*Total Time 40 Minutes*

*Serves 4*

*Ingredients*

1/3 cup erythritol

1 teaspoon xanthan gum

4 egg yolks

2 teaspoons vanilla extract or 1 vanilla bean pod

1 cup thickened cream

1/2 cup almond milk

*Directions*

1. Mix the thickened cream and almond milk in a medium saucepan.

2. Split the vanilla bean in half lengthways with a sharp knife. Scrape out and discard the seeds using the back of the knife.

3. Add in vanilla seeds to the almond milk mixture and bring the ingredients to a simmer, while stirring continuously until hot, or for approximately 5 minutes.

4. Once done, remove the mixture in the saucepan from heat.

5. In a separate bowl, whisk in erythritol, xanthan gum and egg yolks and then pour the milk mixture over the egg yolks. Whisk the mixture continuously.

6. Return the mixture to the saucepan and cook while stirring continuously until the mixture can easily stick to the back of a spoon, or for approximately 15 to 20 minutes.

7. Serve the custard warm or cold.

*Calories 250, Carbs 5g, Protein 4g, Fat 24g*

# Keto Custard - Vanilla Flavor

*Prep Time 15 minutes*

*Cook Time 5 minutes*

*Total Time 20 minutes*

*Servings 5*

*Ingredients*

1 pinch salt

2 teaspoons vanilla extract or 1 Vanilla Bean

2 tablespoons granulated sweetener

6 egg yolks

2 cups heavy whipping cream

*Directions*

1. Start by slicing the vanilla bean in half and use the back of the knife to scrape out the seeds from the bean.

2. Add in the vanilla bean, salt and heavy whipping cream to a small pan. Heat the saucepan over medium heat until it is just boiling, making sure that you stir it now and again.

3. Remove the mixture from heat. Meanwhile in a small bowl whisk together the sweetener and the egg yolks until well blended.

4. Gently add the hot vanilla and creamy mixture over your egg yolk mixture while whisking constantly.

5. Return the mixture to a saucepan and cook over medium low heat until the thick mixture can stick to the back of a spoon, while stirring constantly.

6. Remove the custard from heat and strain it to remove the vanilla pod and any other remaining lumps.

*Calories 400, Carbs 3g, Protein 5g, Fat 41g*

## Low Carb Vanilla Pudding

*Prep Time 5 minutes*

*Cook Time 10 minutes*

*Total Time 15 minutes*

*Serves 6*

*Ingredients*

3 large egg yolks

2 large eggs

1 pinch salt

1 tablespoon cornstarch

1/3 cup Swerve Granulated

1/2 cup almond milk

1 cup heavy cream

3/4 teaspoon gelatin powder

2 tablespoons butter

1/4 teaspoon stevia glycerite

1 teaspoon vanilla

*Directions*

1. In a small pot, bring almond milk and heavy cream to a simmer over medium heat.

2. Put all the dry ingredients apart from cornstarch and erythritol into a heat-safe bowl and whisk them together.

3. Add the egg yolks to the mixture and whisk together. Follow with whole eggs and then whisk again.

4. Put a sieve near the bowl and sprinkle a little gelatin over the tablespoon of water.

5. As soon as the cream is hot and bubbles around the side of the pot, gently pour it into the egg yolk mixture while whisking constantly until well blended.

6. Pour this mixture into the pot and put it over medium low heat. Constantly whisk the mixture until it starts to thicken up, or for approximately 5 minutes.

7. Now turn the heat down a tad and whisk again continuously for another 1 to 2 minutes.

8. Remove the mixture from heat and whisk for another one minute. Put the sieve over the bowl and now pour the vanilla pudding through to remove any little bits of cooked eggs.

9. Whisk in vanilla, butter and the stevia glycerite, taste and adjust the seasoning you like.

10. Add in gelatin and whisk yet again until the gelatin has dissolved and has blended well with the mixture.

11. Cover the pudding with plastic wrap and keep it refrigerated for more than 8 hours, or preferably overnight.

12. Once ready to serve, simply whip the pudding using a hand mixer to ensure it's of a light texture. Enjoy!

*Calories 235, Carbs 3g, Protein 4g, Fat 23g*

# Conclusion

We have come to the end of the book. Thank you for reading and congratulations for reading until the end.

If you found the book valuable, can you recommend it to others? One way to do that is to post a review on Amazon.

# Do You Like My Book & Approach To Publishing?

If you like my writing and style and would love the ease of learning literally everything you can get your hands on from Fantonpublishers.com, I'd really need you to do me either of the following favors.

## 1: First, I'd Love It If You Leave a Review of This Book on Amazon.

## 2: Check Out My Other Keto Diet Books

KETOGENIC DIET: Keto Diet Made Easy: Beginners Guide on How to Burn Fat Fast With the Keto Diet (Including 100+ Recipes That You Can Prepare Within 20 Minutes)- New Edition

KETOGENIC DIET: Ketogenic Diet Recipes That You Can Prepare Using 7 Ingredients and Less in Less Than 30 Minutes

Ketogenic Diet: With A Sustainable Twist: Lose Weight Rapidly With Ketogenic Diet Recipes You Can Make Within 25 Minutes

Ketogenic Diet: Keto Diet Breakfast Recipes

Fat Bombs: Keto Fat Bombs: 50+ Savory and Sweet Ketogenic Diet Fat Bombs That You MUST Prepare Before Any Other!

**Snacks: Keto Diet Snacks: 50+ Savory and Sweet Ketogenic Diet Snacks That You MUST Prepare Before Any Other!**

**Desserts: Keto Diet Desserts: 50+ Savory and Sweet Ketogenic Diet Desserts That You MUST Prepare Before Any Other!**

**Ketogenic Diet: Ketogenic Diet Lunch and Dinner Recipes**

**Ketogenic Diet: Keto Diet Cookbook For Vegetarians**

**Ketogenic Diet: Ketogenic Slow Cooker Cookbook: Keto Slow Cooker Recipes That You Can Prepare Using 7 Ingredients Or Less**

**Note:** This list may not represent all my Keto diet books. You can check the full list by visiting my Author Central: amazon.com/author/fantonpublishers or my website http://www.fantonpublishers.com

**Get updates when we publish any book on the Ketogenic diet: http://bit.ly/2fantonpubketo**

Closely related to the keto diet is intermittent fasting. I also publish books on Intermittent Fasting.

One of the books is shown below:

**Intermittent Fasting: A Complete Beginners Guide to Intermittent Fasting For Weight Loss, Increased Energy, and A Healthy Life**

**Get updates when we publish any book on intermittent fasting:** http://bit.ly/2fantonbooksIF

To get a list of all my other books, please fantonwriters.com, my author central or let me send you the list by requesting them below: http://bit.ly/2fantonpubnewbooks

# 3: Let's Get In Touch

**Antony**

**Website**: http://www.fantonpublishers.com/

**Email:** Support@fantonpublishers.com

**Twitter**: https://twitter.com/FantonPublisher

**Facebook Page**: https://www.facebook.com/Fantonpublisher/

**My Ketogenic Diet Books Page:** https://www.facebook.com/pg/Fast-Keto-Meals-336338180266944

**Private Facebook Group For Readers:** https://www.facebook.com/groups/FantonPublishers/

**Pinterest**: https://www.pinterest.com/fantonpublisher/

# 4: Grab Some Freebies On Your Way Out; Giving Is Receiving, Right?

I gave you 2 freebies at the start of the book, one on general life transformation and one about the Ketogenic diet. Grab them here if you didn't grab them earlier.

**Ketogenic Diet Freebie**: http://bit.ly/2fantonpubketo

**5 Pillar Life Transformation Checklist**: http://bit.ly/2fantonfreebie

## 5: Suggest Topics That You'd Love Me To Cover To Increase Your Knowledge Bank.

I am looking forward to seeing your suggestions and insights; you could even suggest improvements to this book. Simply send me a message on Support@fantonpublishers.com.

# PSS: Let Me Also Help You Save Some Money!

If you are a heavy reader, have you considered subscribing to Kindle Unlimited? You can read this and millions of other books for just $9.99 a month)! You can check it out by searching for Kindle Unlimited on Amazon!

Printed in Great Britain
by Amazon